NEW PERCEPTIONS
P.O. BOX 166
WILLIMANTIC, CT 06226

D0451903

Survival Handbook

for the newly recovering

Scott Sheperd, Ph.D.

CompCare® Publishers
2415 Annapolis Lane
Minneapolis, Minnesota 55441

Published in the United States
by CompCare Publishers.

Sheperd, Scott, 1945–
    Survival handbook for the newly recovering / Scott Sheperd.
        p.   cm.
    ISBN 0-89638-149-8 : $3.95
    1. Alcoholics—Rehabilitation. 2. Narcotic addicts—
Rehabilitation. 3. Alcoholics—Life skills guides. 4. Narcotic
addicts—Life skills guides. I. Title.
HV5275.S45   1988   88-18916
613.8—dc19   CIP

Cover design and interior illustrations by Susan Rinek.

Inquiries, orders, and catalog requests should be addressed to
CompCare Publishers
2415 Annapolis Lane
Minneapolis, Minnesota 55441
Call toll free 800/328-3330
(Minnesota residents 559-4800)

 5   4   3   2   1
92 91 90 89 88

Contents

The Beginning

When you begin your life over without drugs and alcohol, you begin a new journey. For many of you this can be a time of apprehension, fear, and uncertainty. The territory is unfamiliar and you don't know what you need or what to expect. You are a stranger in a new land.

This Survival Handbook for the Newly Recovering can be your map through this new territory and a help in emergency situations along the way. Although the territory is new to you, it is not totally uncharted. Many people have made this trip before you, and their experiences shine like a beacon to guide new travelers.

As you become more familiar with the territory, you will learn that you have many resources available to you, especially within yourself. Using these resources, you will be able to find the courage, strength, and hope to move forward on your way to a place of serenity, acceptance, and satisfaction.

Keep in mind that this handbook is not a substitute for support programs such as AA, DAA, CA, or NA. It is one more source of suggestions for your recovery journey.

1

The Desert of
Low Self-esteem

For many people, beginning a journey into sobriety is overwhelming. The familiar signposts of alcohol and other drugs are missing. Travelers face a harsh, bare desert they don't understand or feel comfortable in. Because they are confused, people often give up when what they need to survive is right at their fingertips. People who are successful in crossing this wilderness are aware that a better life awaits them on the other side.

Whether or not you are successful in your sobriety journey depends on your attitude, strengths, preparation, willingness to work, and ability to recognize the elements of survival. If all you see in front of you is a barren, lifeless

existence, you will relapse and wither. If you see
the quality of life that surrounds you, your
chances of survival are much greater.

To increase chances for survival successful travelers bring their support systems on the journey
with them—they don't try to make it alone. Your
preparation consists of what you have learned in
treatment, AA, and any other support systems you
are using. This is survival training of the highest
order.

Desert Survival Strategies

Your preparation for crossing the desert must be
twofold: You need to increase your awareness of
the good life waiting for you out in the world, and
you need to get rid of the desert inside yourself.

People with low self-esteem may have trouble
doing this. Very few people can change old,
negative thought patterns overnight. You may
decide to seek professional help. Also these survival strategies will come in handy. Read them
carefully and try to do what they say.

1. *First, believe that you are worth the effort it
   takes to make this journey.* Without this basic
   belief, you will quit, and when you quit, you

will die—maybe not a physical death, but certainly a spiritual and emotional death.

To stimulate this positive belief in yourself, try accepting these thoughts:

- You matter because you are *you!*
- You have potential. You make a difference.
- You can help other people just by being you.

Don't just dismiss these thoughts because you are having trouble believing them right this moment. Be patient. It is better to be telling yourself these things than the old you-are-a-loser message. It may help you to write down these new messages daily.

Don't accept society's message that you are worth something only when you have accomplished certain things. Of course, accomplishing something you want to accomplish will help you feel better about yourself. It reinforces the idea that you are capable of expanding your limits and learning new skills.

But if you haven't accomplished much lately because of dependence on alcohol and drugs, don't believe you are less of a person. It is the process of attempting to achieve that is the mark of a person with courage. You are attempting to achieve ongoing quality sobriety. That says a lot about your quality as a person. You do matter. You do have courage. Just being on this journey of sobriety is proof of that.

Tell yourself: "What I accomplish does not make me worthwhile. I accomplish those things because I already am worthwhile."

2. If you have trouble seeing your good qualities, *follow the suggestions in the strength assessment inventory* in this Survival Handbook. If you have difficulty completing it by yourself, ask someone you trust to help you finish it.

3. *Get yourself in shape for this trip physically and spiritually.*

   • Get some exercise. You don't have to become a world class runner, but walk or run or swim or do anything that requires physical effort.

   • Try to eat well-balanced meals.

   • Get your body back in touch with the world. Don't just pass through. Examine a leaf. Touch a flower. Take time to look at, touch, and feel the things around you.

   • Get your spirit back in touch with the world. You may have lost sight of the bigger picture. You may be unaware of your bond with the planet.

   Your spirit, crippled by alcohol and drugs, needs to be nurtured and allowed to heal. Old messages and attitudes from your old life need to be replaced by new ones. Look for new ideas in your support groups.

Become aware of how you are linked to other people. Look at people not just in terms of who they are or what you can get from them, but as your companions on this journey.

4. *Keep an open mind, open to all possibilities for help and support.* The more rigid you are the less likely you will be to make adjustments when you need to. If, for example, you refuse to go to AA or other support group meetings because you think they are weird or you're uncomfortable being there, you are no smarter than the man who dies of thirst on the desert because there's no bottled sparkling water around.

- One way to keep an open mind is to expose yourself to new ideas. Read what other people have to say about life. You don't have to agree with them, but at least examine some different views. Expand your notions of what is *possible.*

- Meet new people and get different viewpoints. Support groups are a wonderful source of information, experience, and wisdom. Again, you don't have to agree with everyone, but at least listen to them.

- When you disagree with someone, attempt to see the other's point of view. Don't just dismiss his or her ideas as stupid.

- Reexamine the way you look at things and ideas and people. What habits of thought have you fallen into? Is your attitude helping you grow, increasing your wisdom, creating good, strong positive relationships? Is your way of looking at things helping you have a quality sobriety? Take an action to change if you need to.

5. *Besides an open mind, you need an open heart if you are going to survive your journey.*
   - Listen to your heart. What do you really want? Are you lonely? Is love missing from your life? Get in touch with your feelings. You need to know what you are looking for.

   - Don't put your heart in a box. Many people don't ask for emotional support because they don't want to be a burden or look like they are begging for love. Sometimes they are so afraid of being rejected that they avoid reaching out and opening up.

   - Let other people care for you. Don't push people away because you are afraid they will push you away. There are many caring people ready to support you if you let them. If one or two try to manipulate you or take advantage of you, you can survive them. Don't let them stop you from meeting and getting to know the people who care.

- An open heart is also one that is willing to give. Don't just focus on what you need but look around and find out what others need. Try to help them if you can. Give away what you are receiving from sobriety.

6. *Keep educating yourself on the effects of alcohol and other drugs.* Books, movies, and lectures are sources. Listen to the stories of other recovering people.

7. *Create something.* Many people don't see themselves as creative because they haven't written a hit song or a symphony or they haven't painted a great masterpiece. Creativity is an attitude, a way of interacting with life, the discovery of new effective answers to old problems. Write down the ways you are creative in your day-to-day life. If you have trouble doing this, ask for help from someone who knows you.

   The more creative you are the more options you can see. For a person attempting to restructure his or her life without alcohol and drugs, options are critical for survival. Besides, being creative can be fun.

- Write a journal about your experiences.
- Try your hand at poetry or writing a song.
- Paint a picture or build something.

8. *Find out where your nourishment is going to
come from once you get out on the desert.* One
major source is your support system, which may
include family, friends, AA, treatment programs,
EAP programs, school counselors, psycholo-
gists, and clergy. There are many nourishing
oases out on the desert. Find them and help
yourself.

- If you are one of those "I don't need any-
  body" or "I can take care of myself" people,
  you'll have to change your thinking or be
  prepared to be very thirsty on the desert.

- Also, you can't just use the resources without
  giving something back. If everyone on this
  trip did nothing but use what was available,
  the resources would be used up. Others have
  given back and so must you. Get involved
  with your support group—maybe something
  as simple as cleaning ashtrays or greeting
  people. Let your friends know you care about
  them and then support them when they need
  help. Help young people who want alcohol-
  and drug-free lives.

- Sometimes a resource is just out of sight, and
  you have to look hard to find it. For example,
  in a strained relationship with a parent or
  spouse, all you and the other person may see
  are the negative aspects when just below the
  surface is a great deal of love and support.

Both of you may not know how to reach that love because it is buried under the fear of being rejected or hurt. Be patient and supportive and perhaps slowly that love will surface. You both may need help in this process. Ask for it.

- Digging through anger and resentments and fear—both your own and others—to get to love and caring calls for forgiveness. Be willing to forgive yourself and others. Let go of the pain and cut through the pride and arrogance that often block forgiveness. Accept yourself and others as you are, where you are today. Accept the fact that we all screw up sometimes. We are not saints. If you keep trying to be perfect or expect others to be, you are wasting your energy. People on this sobriety journey cannot afford to waste energy.

Assess Your Strengths

To get through the tough situations on your journey, you need to know your strengths and build your survival skills on them. This inventory will help you explore those strengths. You are encouraged to get some paper and list what the following sections ask for. Don't send yourself on this trip toward a quality sobriety without knowing what you are capable of and what you have going for you.

Personal Characteristics

Look for things about yourself that you see as positive, for example, a sense of humor, loyalty, kindness, dependability, good listening skills. It doesn't matter that these traits are not as outstanding as you might like them to be, or that some of them disappeared when you were drinking or using. If you show some of them some of the time and they are important to you, write them down as strengths. If you have trouble coming up with a list, ask some friends to tell you what they see as positive about you.

Positive Personal Habits

Write down the things you do for yourself every day that you probably pay little attention to. For example, let's say that you brush your teeth regularly. You probably say, "So what? Most people do." But people who have quit believing in themselves, who see life as pointless and dreary don't even do the little things for themselves. Small habits like taking a shower, washing your hair, and eating good food show that you still care for yourself.

Accomplishments
We're not talking about winning a tennis trophy
or a quiz show contest. We mean *anything* that
you worked for and accomplished: building a
table, solving a puzzle, losing weight, raising a
grade, standing up for yourself. Look back over
your whole life—even to your childhood. No
accomplishment is too small. Everything counts.
List them all.

Efforts to Accomplish
Write down those things you tried to do but for
whatever reason didn't. This could mean starting
something but not finishing, or setting some goal
such as losing so many pounds and not reaching
it. Or it could be something like quitting smoking
and then relapsing. *The point is not that you
failed but that you tried.* Your goals show you
what is important to you and what you can still
achieve if you want to. They also show that you
can survive setbacks and failures. You are not a
failure because you failed at something. If you
don't make the attempt, you give up on life. You
decide how much effort you will put into this
journey. Remembering your previous efforts can
be very helpful on the journey ahead.

Skills
We may overlook our skills because we don't think
they are very important. For example, most people

would see being a carpenter or playing the piano as skills. But there are other skills such as being a good listener, telling jokes, motivating people, organizing things, calming people down, and many others. List anything you do that is useful, helpful, or just fun. You don't have to make money from it for it to be a skill.

Individual Events
What actions have you taken in your life that you feel positive about? At first some may seem insignificant (such as, "picked up a package someone dropped" or "told someone I'm sorry"). Others may seem more important, such as "supported my friend when his father died" or "paid back the money I owed." The only requirement is that you feel positive about something you did. Go back as far as you can remember. Even if you haven't done many things recently that you feel good about, the earlier events will remind you of what you can do.

If at first these exercises feel silly or a waste of time, ask yourself if you really know your strengths and if your self-esteem is really very high. It helps you more to look for the good in yourself than to wallow in the misery. Remember, your sobriety and your life depend on how much you value yourself.

2

The Swamp of Boredom

One of the most dangerous places you may have to pass through is the swamp of boredom. People who linger too long in this swamp eventually become trapped. Slowly they sink until nothing is left.

Alcohol and drugs make the swamp of boredom one of their regular haunts. They promise a way out to travelers seeking release from boredom. Don't be fooled by false promises. Learn to recognize when you are getting close to the swamp and take action.

Recognizing the Outer Edges of the Swamp

Many people don't see that they are having problems with boredom until they are caught in the middle of the swamp, and then it is extremely difficult to get out. The earlier you understand what is happening, the quicker you will be able to make changes. Here are some warning signs:

1. Are you paying less and less attention to what you are doing?
   - Staring at TV but not watching it.
   - Daydreaming a lot.
   - Not listening to what people are saying.
   - Losing interest in what you're reading.

2. Are you becoming more restless?
   - Pacing.
   - Opening the refrigerator and staring in but not being hungry.
   - Feeling lots of energy but having no place to put it.

3. Do you feel more lethargic—very little energy?
   - Finding it difficult to do the simplest task.
   - Feeling weighted down.

- Being entertained only in a passive way, like watching TV or movies or listening to the radio. Not participating, just observing.

4. Are you constantly reminiscing about the fun you had when you were drinking or using?

   - Talking over old times with people still drinking and using, and enjoying the memories.

   - Visiting old places where the good times happened during the drug and alcohol days.

   - Turning down opportunities to do fun things without drugs by saying they sound boring.

   - Looking at people who are not using or drinking and seeing them as boring and dull.

5. Are you beginning to ask yourself "Who cares?" or "What's the difference?"

6. Are you beginning to equate sobriety with boredom?

7. Are you finding yourself doing the same thing day after day and week after week?

8. Are your relationships not satisfying?

   - Finding yourself wanting to spend more time with the users you know.

- Constantly looking for flaws in those people you know who don't use or drink.

- Envying other's relationships and thinking how rotten yours are compared to theirs.

9. Are you looking for someone or something to take your boredom away?

10. Do you avoid meeting new people, getting involved with new organizations, doing anything new that could be fun or educational or stimulating?

11. Are you getting away from support groups and support people?

If you answered Yes to any of these questions, you could be moving into the swamp of boredom. If you answered Yes to many of these questions, you are already deep into the swamp.

Take the first step to get out now.

Getting Out of the Swamp

1. Go to your support group meetings. Increase the number if you need to. Call for rides if you have to, but get there.

2. Get involved in your support groups. Besides the meetings, go to the extra activities they offer, like dances and picnics.

3. Call your sponsor and other supportive people both in and out of the recovery program.

4. Use the Boredom Escape Strategies below to aid you in escaping the swamp.

5. Remember your value as a human being—one who can care about others and give to others.

6. Take a hard look at your attitude. Are you like the little kid who says he won't like something before he even tries it?

7. Keep an open mind.

8. Don't be seduced by how easy it is to make fun of people who don't use chemicals, or activities that don't involve chemicals.

9. Sit by a river or a mountain, or anywhere in nature, and just watch and listen. Learn from the land. Life is not boring. It is magical! Open your eyes.

10. Get active in the entertainment side of your life—whether it be arts or sports or reading. (Yes, reading is active—for the imagination above all.)

11. Believe that you can get out of the swamp sober and alive.

12. Reach into your soul and tap the power that is there. You have power.

13. Break your routines. Remember the only difference between a rut and a grave is the depth.

14. Take healthy risks instead of the old type you used to take. Share feelings, apply for a new job, assert yourself, take a self-inventory.

15. Don't wait until you are in the middle of the swamp to start implementing the ideas given here.

16. Listen to records or tapes that may help motivate you and stimulate enthusiasm for your new way of living.

17. Remember, new friends and new ideas are waiting for you in your support groups and in the rest of your life. Don't be tricked by the offer of help from drugs and alcohol.

Boredom Escape Strategies

1. Write down your schedule for an entire typical week. Be detailed. Break it down into five-minute groupings if you have to.

2. Find when you are most bored: the time of day, day of the week, activities you are doing when bored, people you are with. Be a detective.

3. Write down any clues you pick up from this list. You may see a pattern. Then determine what changes you can make immediately that might eliminate some boredom. Don't say there aren't any. Remember boredom is a major cause of relapse.

4. Make a list of activities (A) you like to do and still do regularly, (B) you like to do but only do rarely, (C) you used to like to do but haven't done in a long time and (D) you think you might be interested in but haven't explored.

5. Keep doing (A). Do more of (B). Start doing (C) again. Begin exploring how to get involved in (D).

6. Think up ways to spend your time more effectively and enjoyably. Write them down. If you are having trouble with answers, talk to people in the program or other friends who don't find the answers in drugs and alcohol. Take a chance by going with them on one of these activities. See if you like it before dismissing it as a possibility.

7. Make a list of friends who are not a threat to your sobriety, including your new friends in AA, NA, or other support groups. Most people are not ready to abandon *all* their old friends, no matter what anyone tells them, but make an effort to be selective. Find people who are alive spiritually and emotionally and who are excited about being alive.

8. Besides making a list, *make contact* with those friends who support you as a person. Share your activities with them.

9. Break your routines. Notice which shoe you put on first in the morning. Put the other one on first. Go to work or school by different routes. Sit in different seats at meetings. Eat at different times if possible. Eat different foods. When you get home, change your normal pattern. Go for a walk instead of watching

TV. Look at all the routines you have and see if you can modify them even just a little. Develop new routines that encourage creativity, happiness, and a sense of involvement.

10. Write down all the skills you have, even ones you don't use regularly. Ask your friends to help you. Many times people have skills they don't even know about. Once you recognize your skills, figure out ways to use them to put challenge and excitement into your life.

3

The Cold Wind of Loneliness

Besides the desert and swamp you may face on your journey, an unseen danger can stop you dead in your tracks. It can paralyze you and take away your will to live. It can take the color out of your life and give you back an empty shell. It is the cold wind of loneliness.

Once again drugs and alcohol wait patiently. They have offered warmth and comfort before, and they remind you how nice it was when they were your best "friends."

Don't be fooled by false memories. You can also remember how alone and isolated you felt when you were drinking and using. Remind yourself that the chemicals offer a false warmth, one that fades quickly and leaves you even more vulnerable to the cold and the wind.

Take a stand against loneliness now.

Loneliness Survival Strategies

1. Remember, you have you. If you are not your own friend, you will always be lonely. Remind yourself that you make a difference.

2. Write down what you think would make you not lonely. If this requires other people to do things differently or situations to somehow change, you may feel lonely for a long time. Remember, you can't control others—how they think or act. You can only control you. Don't waste your energy trying to talk others into building your fire. Build it yourself.

3. Now write down what *you* can do to help yourself not be lonely. Think back to a time when you weren't lonely (without chemicals) and find out what made that happen. Talk to others and ask them what they do to warm up and fight the loneliness.

4. Wrap yourself in the warmth of those who love you and care about you. Your family, friends, and fellow recoverers are there. They will help you survive the coldest nights.

5. Learn how to use the energy of the sun. Try getting close to nature. Sit by a river again.

Hike a trail. Take a canoe ride. Watch the life in a tidepool. Notice the sky. The loneliness will go. Be a solar cell. Take the warmth of life and make it work for you.

6. If you find you can't fight off the cold and the wind, get help. See a counselor, psychologist, minister—someone you trust with some professional skills. A little help now can make a big difference later.

4

The Smoldering Heat of Resentment

In addition to the cold wind of loneliness, you may have to deal with the boiling heat of resentment as you travel toward sobriety. This feeling simmers and smolders, building up slowly at first but eventually immobilizing its victim, making further progress impossible. The person is literally consumed.

As always, alcohol and drugs promise quick relief. But turning to chemicals is like pouring gasoline on a fire. The resentments do not go away, but build quickly and explode.

Take an action now to beat the heat of resentment.

Beat the Heat Strategies

1. Let your support groups provide shade to protect you from the heat. Learn from them with your head and your heart.

2. Blow the hot air out of your ego. The bigger the ego the hotter the resentment. If "How dare they wrong *me*!" is the essence of your life, you are going to burn out fast.

3. Ask yourself if resentments are helping your life. Are you better off feeling resentful? Are you more fulfilled? Is resentment helping you stay sober?

4. Quit telling yourself you have a right to feel resentful because of how you were treated. There is nothing worse than a self-righteous martyr. Think about it. Are you saying you deserve to feel miserable? That's not saying much for yourself.

5. Catch the cooling breeze of forgiveness. Forgiveness blows away resentment and allows the spirit to heal.

6. Learn to let go. It takes more energy to hold on to something than to let go. Once you let

go, you are ready to take on something new
and healthy.

7. Block out the destroying heat with a shield of
   love. If your life is motivated by love, there
   will be no room for resentment. This does not
   have to be romantic love. It can be the love of
   a person who cares about life and wants to be
   a vital part of it.

8. Jump into the refreshing waters of enthusiasm.
   Enthusiasm looks at today and tomorrow.
   Resentment is lost in yesterday. Enthusiasm
   energizes. Resentment deadens.

9. Ask yourself how many people might be wasting time feeling resentful about the you who
   used to use chemicals. Even though you have
   changed, they may still be caught up hating the
   old you.

10. Picture this day as your last on earth. Would
    you want to spend your last moments hating,
    resentful, bitter?

11. Resentment goes directly against the idea of
    "A Day at a Time" because you're bringing
    old days along for the ride. The burden will
    kill you.

5

The Mountains of Depression

When the mountains of depression first loom
on the horizon, many newly recovering people are
dismayed. They thought that once they stopped
drinking and using, depression would be gone for
good. They thought that the joy of their new
sobriety would carry them through the rest of
life's problems. They forgot that people can have
problems even when chemicals are not involved.

When they begin the climb over the mountains
of depression, many recovering people become
exhausted and disoriented and are finally over-
come. They are not prepared for how steep it is.
At some point they may see a rescue team of
alcohol and drugs which promises them a fast way
over the mountains. Unless exposed as the menace
it is, this rescue team will lead climbers into a

hidden, deep valley. To survive, they will then have to struggle just to get back to where they were in the first place. Many people never survive this "rescue."

Don't be fooled. Instead call on your resources. Use this guide when you are at the bottom or starting your climb.

A Guide through the Mountains

1. Don't focus on how low you are and how high the mountains seem. This can be a trick of perception. There may be many paths that will take you safely through the mountains. Focus on what is right around you—the people and ideas that can help you through.

2. If you are feeling totally lost, get help from a psychologist, psychiatrist or counselor, or from a minister or someone you trust in your support group. But get help! If you isolate yourself, you will surely stay lost.

3. Make sure you have the proper tools to make it over the mountains. You need first of all a desire to stay clean and sober. You also need

courage, strength, self-discipline, humor, humility, high self-esteem, the ability to ask for help, your support group, an open mind, and don't forget love for others and for yourself.

4. Notice the beauty around you. The hardest mountains to climb have the most magnificent views. How you see your situation is a critical factor in how you handle your climb.

5. Don't give up! At times you may feel, "What's the use? I can't do it." Reach down deep inside yourself and find the power to continue. Every great champion has found that extra reserve. Making it over the mountains of depression takes the heart and spirit of a champion.

6. Watch for the phony "rescue team" of alcohol and drugs. There will be times when they look good. They will promise shortcuts to happiness and contentment. Remember where you came from when you were not sober.

7. Be prepared. Not everyone in recovery goes through depression, but many do. In fact, depression is often a normal phase of recovery. Don't think that you are immune. Don't be naive and think there will be no more problems now that the chemicals are gone.

8. An accurate map can be critical to your survival. People in your support group have maps of their own paths and will freely share them. You can learn from them. But you still have to make the trip yourself and be willing to revise their maps and discover your own path.

Paths out of Depression

Choose your own path and follow it. Although there are many paths through the mountains of depression, they are overgrown with resistance. You will have to work hard to break through the barriers. Keep your eyes on the trail or you will lose your way. The paths described here are not the only ones available to lead you out of the mountains. Perhaps you will find a totally new one. But even after you find the path, you aren't out of the woods. *You* still must make the trip.

Professional Help
Many people stuck in depression need to get help from a professional mental health person such as a psychologist, psychiatrist, counselor, etc. It is not a sign of craziness on your part if you see a professional. Many of you will not need this very long anyway. A reputable professional is not

interested in extending treatment for more money. Before you start with someone, see if you can get recommendations from people you trust. Remember, you can always switch therapists if you are not happy. Make sure, however, you are not changing just to avoid the hard work the trail demands.

Challenges
One way to break through depression is to challenge yourself. Do something new. Meet new people. Take a class. Although you risk not succeeding at everything you try, just the experience of the challenge will help you break through depression.

Support Groups
Don't forget your support groups such as AA, NA, DAA, CA, and others. Members can tell you how they dealt with feelings like yours. These are caring, loving human beings who are staying sober and having fun. Get involved with them and the mountains of depression will fade away.

Communicating Feelings
Don't hold your feelings inside. Find someone to share what you are going through. This doesn't mean that you just sit around and complain. You can be sharing good as well as bad feelings. Being

open means asking for others' ideas about what
you are doing, thinking and feeling. You might
not always like what you hear, but you are keeping
yourself open. People who are depressed often
retreat into themselves. Try not to do that.

Relationships

Develop relationships—all kinds. Don't wait for
the "right" ones to come along. Go out and start
them. Remember, satisfying relationships don't
have to be sexual or intense. They can be casual
and informal.

But if you want a real relationship you need to
contribute part of yourself. When you're
depressed, you often don't want to contribute or
don't think you have much to contribute. Keep
telling yourself that idea is wrong. Give even when
you don't feel like it. When you're depressed, you
never feel like giving. Give anyway.

Higher Power

The path of a Higher Power is very different for
different people, but for everyone a Higher Power
is a source of strength. How you define that
strength is up to you, but drawing on that source
of power can be critical to beating depression.
This Power can serve as a constant internal guide
through the mountains and a resource that will get
you out of depression and into serenity.

One thing common to all these paths—and to others you may find—is the need to *get involved*. Just as in sobriety you had to move from thinking about doing something about the chemicals to actually doing something, in depression you operate the same way. Just thinking about climbing won't get you started through the mountains. You need to act—even when you don't feel like it.

Take an action now to survive!

6

Onward

If you have been abusing alcohol and/or other drugs and are now trying to live your life without them, you must realize that you are fighting for your life—physically, spiritually, and emotionally. Approach your quest for sobriety with a healthy respect for the power and seductiveness of the chemicals that will kill you if you let them. But even more important, believe that you have the internal and external resources to live a day at a time without alcohol or drugs.

The feelings mentioned in this handbook are not the only feelings that can impede your journey to sobriety. The strategies given here for sobriety are not the only ones. But they are critical feelings and important strategies. If you succeed in raising your self-esteem and coping with the feelings of depression, resentment, loneliness, and boredom, you will be a long way toward an ongoing sobriety.

If you use the strategies given in this handbook as a supplement to the strategies given in AA, NA, CA, and treatment programs, you will be putting together a blueprint for a drug- and alcohol-free life.

Life can be joyous and free or full of constant pain and misery. Only you can determine the direction your life takes. Only you can choose.

Guideposts

Notes to Myself along the Way

As you travel toward a more secure and happy recovery, there will be many important things you'll want to remember—people who support you (and their phone numbers), group meetings (times and places), activities which always help, inspirational quotes, and more. These vital guideposts are your personal survival tools. Record them on the following pages.

Notes

Notes

Notes

Notes

Notes

Notes

Notes

Notes

Notes

About the Author:

Scott Sheperd, Ph.D., Director of the
Training Institute at Flower Memorial Hospi-
tal in Sylvania, Ohio, has worked in the area
of chemical dependency for about ten years,
both with adults and adolescents. Currently
his major interest is in prevention, both for
the person who has never used and for the
person who has quit using.